Wednesday: New and Selected Poems

For Corey –
Happy 30th Birthday!

WEDNESDAY:
New and Selected Poems

Laurel Blossom

The Writers Voice
&
Ridgeway Press
2004

Copyright © 2004 by Laurel Blossom

ISBN 1-56439-122-1

First Edition

I would like to thank *American Poetry Review, Caprice, Columbia, Heliotrope, Light: A Quarterly of Light Verse, lips, Many Mountains Moving, New York Quarterly, The Paris Review, Pequod, Poetry, Seneca Review*, and online, www.BigCityLit.com, www.winningwriters.com, and www.poetz.com, where some of these poems were first published. Some of these poems were written with the help of grants from the Ohio Arts Council, the New York Foundation for the Arts, the National Endowment for the Arts, and fellowships from Yaddo and Harris Manchester College, Oxford University. I would like to thank these institutions for their encouragement and support. My everlasting thanks to family and friends who have offered moral support over many years, including my husband, Leonard Todd; my daughter, Becca Kovacik; my brothers Charles Bingham Blossom and Dudley Stuart Blossom, their wives Debbie and Kay, and their children; my sister Elizabeth Meers and her family; my dear friends Suzanne Bennett, Kathy Berlowe, Connie Berry, Susan Charlotte, Linda Corrente, Susan Crowder, Laura deBoisblanc, Cheri Fein, Anne Heller, Cleo McNelly Kearns, Maura Kelly, Jane Gregory Rubin, Nell Gilmore Stanley, and Nancy Wolitzer; and my colleagues Daryln Brewer, David Evanier, Robin Hirsch, Amy Holman, M.L. Liebler, Tom Lux, Cleopatra Mathis, Carol Muske-Dukes, Jason Shinder, Angelo Verga, and Barry Wallenstein, among so many others. And thanks to Irving Berlin for several poem titles—L. B.

The type is Baskerville, based on the types of John Baskerville, a distinguished eighteenth-century English printer and typefounder.
Book design by Gary Metras

Ridgeway Press
P.O. Box 120
Roseville, MI 48066

The Writers Voice of the YMCA of Metropolitan Detroit
a member of the National Writer's Voice Project
of the YMCA of the USA

For Jason

Contents

WEDNESDAY: NEW POEMS

MORBID FASCINATION ... 11
MY VOICE WAS CHANGING ... 12
GREENVILLE HIGH DRESS CODE ... 13
FATHER'S DAY ... 14
I'LL TELL YOU NO LIE ... 15
THE NEAR OCCASION OF SIN ... 16
HOW MUCH WOULD I CRY ... 18
IN A BLIZZARD LONG AFTER THE EVENTS OF WINTER ... 19
VANISHING POINT ... 20
MY GIRLHOOD ... 23
CRITICS DEBATE THE UNEXPURGATED JOURNALS ... 24
DECEMBER SOLSTICE ... 25
ELEGY IN THE FLESH ... 26
WHERE WERE YOU ... 28
GRIEF ... 31
WHAT HAPPENED AFTER WHAT HAPPENED ... 32
NEW YORK: THE ARGUMENT OF HER BOOKE ... 33
THIRTEEN WAYS OF LOOKING AT MRS. BLACKBIRD ...34
NOT NEARLY THE SONNET SHE'D HAVE WRITTEN HERSELF ... 36
SALLY FIELD HAS A DREAM ABOUT HER MOTHER ... 37
DOUBLE TAKE ... 38
ALMOST BIBLICAL ... 39
HOW HIGH IS THE SKY ... 40
LOUISE GLÜCK'S HAIR ... 41
CUT SHORT ... 42
HOW MUCH DO I LOVE YOU ... 43
GOOD FRIDAY IN UMBRIA ... 44
WHAT BIG TEETH ... 47

FROM *WHAT'S WRONG*

UNDER THE COVERS ... 51
FRIGGINS DIVISION ... 52
SKATE ... 53
FOUND POEM ... 54
DOOMED ... 55
SOMEPLACE HOT ...56
NEXT TIME ... 57
WHAT'S WRONG ... 58
RULES OF THE CONTEST ... 59

FROM *THE PAPERS SAID*

LANDSCAPE PAINTING ... 63
FOR GREGORY, CHUCK AND JOHN ... 64
THE PAPERS SAID ... 65
RADIO ... 67
COMPLAINT ... 70
THE MAN WHO USED TO LIVE IN MY APARTMENT ... 71
NO IS THE ANSWER, THE ANSWER IS NO ... 72

Wednesday: New Poems

Morbid Fascination

If as a boy you lived in a land of women
Languid but for the first flushed moments
Following the latest letter from the Front;

Or, like me: when asked to watch my little sister,
I watched the sled come hurtling toward her
Down the white hill of my fascinated heart;

Maybe, in the aftermath of the execution,
We all feel the urge to work our fingers in
The holes of his body the condemned man loved.

On the ocean floor, where earth's core
Erupts and water does not boil,
Huge sulfur-breathing tube worms, eels, clams

The size of dinner platters,
Red-blooded crabs and mussels dwell,
Who do not need the sun or grace or oxygen at all.

My Voice Was Changing

When I was a boy, I was happy. We lived in the country. I chased cows. I played catch with my brothers. We rode our bikes all over the neighborhood. We dared each other to jump off walls. I had a dog. I brought home snakes and lizards and butterflies in their cocoons and worms for fishing. I went fishing with Eddie. I went deep-sea fishing and I didn't get sick.

That's not true. I got sick. That was the first sign. I stopped climbing trees. I stopped daring kids to climb up on roofs. I read books. My parents gave my dog away. When my sister was born, she sat on my lap. I spent time indoors. I let my hair grow. I didn't shave, though technically I could have. One day, when I looked in the mirror, I had turned into a girl.

Greenville High Dress Code

Student dress and grooming will be neat and clean.
Shoes or sandals will be worn; flip-flops (shower-type shoes) are not permitted.
No bare-midriff shirts or blouses will be allowed.
No tank-, spaghetti strap-, halter-tops, or vests without shirts will be permitted.
Shoulder straps have to be a minimum of 1 inch wide.
No see-through or mesh-type garments may be worn.
Hats, sunglasses, hair curlers, skullies, or do-raps are prohibited.
No clothing or jewelry will be permitted that displays profanity, suggestive phrases, alcohol, tobacco, drug advertisements or other inappropriate phrases or symbols.
Shorts may be worn; however, they must be properly fitted and in good taste and may not be shorter than mid-thigh.
Biker shorts or athletic shorts of any kind are not permitted.
Skirts should fit, be in good taste and not be shorter than mid-thigh.
Clothing that inappropriately exposes underclothing or body parts is unacceptable.
Trousers/slacks/shorts must be worn at waist level.
For safety reasons, excessively baggy trousers and clothing are not permitted.
Non-human colored hair is not permitted.
Clothing may not drag on the floor.
Extraneous articles hanging from clothing, such as chains or other articles, are inappropriate and will not be allowed.
Facial jewelry is permitted to be worn only on the ears.

Father's Day

WQXR is playing something loud, important
trumpets announcing events at court.

I'm in the kitchen, shelling peas, snapping beans,
enjoying it for the first time.

Sitting on a stool whereon is painted
Einstein's face and the black word THINK.

Talking out loud to my mother-in-law-that-was
rolling out pastry dough in Chicago;

to Mary ironing shirts;
to Anna coming home in her muddy hip boots;

to my sister making hospital corners;
to Shirley and Betty and Dawn.

We're crowded into my narrow yellow kitchen,
talking, working, laughing

so hard we're about to die or pee or come,
watching the vegetables pile up one by one,

like casualties or children, raw data
for the awkward questions we're forever raising.

I'll Tell You No Lie

The pink railing reached up just high enough.
Mother stood the three little ones on chairs.

Between the silver ocean and the turquoise bay.
A small crowd gathered just as he said it would.

My father could do terrible things.
He could make his eyes bright with welcoming.

The Near Occasion of Sin

To Miss Marianne Moore

Hairy face, skin wings, eyeteeth of bone, black
thought of it swinging from the chandelier, upside down
    above
me in my bed: *I too dislike it.* I hear whirring
and its squeaky voice in my dreams: it wakes me, years
    after.
He says be grateful, you could be one of the undead. Even so,
To clip the tiny bombs to their blind bodies,
load them by the hundreds

on B-29s, and drop them where the rising sun can warm
    them
as they fall, so they waken like the dream
where you don't hit bottom; then, as if by radar, fly
under eaves, feeding on insects and resting for an hour, until
they explode, little bat-bombs
burning the whole city flat and everybody smoldering
in it: it makes me sick. He says

this never happened, be grateful
the A-bombs bat-bombs were invented to come after, like
    letters
in the alphabet of a new world language, worked: word
    made
flash. Ah, Poetry!
couldst thou make shadows of mine enemies

on walls of Sumitomo Banks and Pentagons, etc., half-lives
decaying in some circle of hell, flapping overhead

or clinging by their little claws
to the one source of firepower in the room: but no,
traitor, you turn me into them, you bite. Even tonight,
when he rolls over to kiss me in his sleep, I shudder
or tremble, thinking of the greener grass that grew
after Hiroshima, the root of our ginger
that scratched through its plastic pot to get at the ground.

How Much Would I Cry

Give up, the weather is working for me now,
confusing our enemies with ingenious disguises,
me as a red-headed woman, winter as spring.
We're all decked out in the very latest
camouflage: yellow, green green.
The process-server is easily identifiable.

You kept one promise, anyhow. I'm not bored.
The jumping-off place for out of your life
is at least as interesting as the place
for jumping in. We crossed a few
useless boundaries in between, but who's counting.
The end of an era isn't always recognizable.

Get out your maps: desert islands is a clue.
If you really want to find me, baby,
play the old standards, tinker with the moon.
You have the champagne, your own private beach,
all that water. Use your imagination.
Replacement parts may not be readily available.

In a Blizzard Long After
the Events of Winter

I wake up married.
Others have parents
spring back to life, whole
wards proliferate
with relapses, neighborhoods
banging for heat.
As if

we all had it all
to do over: white sky
closed like a casket,
diaries blank,
a busload of children
buried in the past,
too deep to be let out.

Vanishing Point

It could almost be called well-worn
except that those who consider this their territory
come and kick dirt and a few broken branches and dead
    leaves

over it, a suggestion –
they don't bother to be systematic. And it works,
temporarily, like staring at the sun, angry

red spots like stop signs, like asking for it, blood
wherever you look, heel marks
of boots too big to be a woman's

sunk deep into the soaking ground, the grass
loves it, world gone green again, then golden.
It's a trick

of light, so intense it feels like vengeance, me
against you, and winning no matter what. All the men
    I know
are like this, enemies in my path. You started it

when we were kids in the woods
you told me I couldn't enter
without the magic words, like my dumb dog

climbing under the neighboring farmer's fence
after he'd warned her two or three times.
She was pregnant.

She hauled herself home full of buckshot
to give birth. Don't tell me she was stealing chickens,
I don't care, you're making it up, how would she know.

Now chain links guard the silence
you used to pitch into, the baseball as it hit
the uneven stones of the front steps

bouncing back at unpredictable angles:
"It's a pop fly, ladies and gents,
moving back, Doby's under it, he's got it,

a spectacular catch, l's and g's, and the side's retired."
Like perspective from the point of view of
disappearance, I look back

from places you never dreamed of—New York, Tokyo,
    Paris, Marrakech—
and I should be happy, but I'm not.
You are. This planet isn't big enough for both of us.

Home is what I want too,
that feeling, but it's always paved over
by the time I get back, sold to a giant corporation

for its intergalactic headquarters. Look, where we're
    standing,
part of a wall's been preserved
for aesthetic reasons, to hide a hole in the earth

the size of the meteorite that doomed the dinosaurs.
That's how I feel exactly. My shrink asks me what's wrong
with despair. I suspect him,

like you, of wanting to watch me suffer.
I would do anything to please him.
We named the one puppy Hoax,

retriever irretrievably allergic to grass
already on the brink of extinction,
brown and burning.

My Girlhood

I could wrap it
for Christmas, like a present
I don't remember
who gave me last year
and give it
back.

I could lay it
in a drawer
like my mother's best
old linen
handkerchief.
I could

let it rot
in silos.
I could corner
the market in
its precious commodity.
One man, walking

two steps behind me,
could carry it
handcuffed to his wrist,
but I haven't quite
picked out
the lucky guy.

Critics Debate the Unexpurgated Journals

He said why did she bake the yellow cake at all, taking time away from her writing.

Then he said her husband was the superior poet, anyway.

She said she wound up having a certain sympathy for the husband.

He said she worked hard. He compared her to Keats. Not, he hastened, to compare great with little.

He said he gave her to his first-year students to study how much can be accomplished through sheer determination.

He said he didn't like the journals, they show her jejune, adolescent, vengeful, and self-absorbed.

She said she also sympathized with the woman.

He said she was pregnant, but never even mentions it.

She said she didn't need to, she was talking to herself.

He said nobody keeps a journal without wanting someone else to read it.

She said yellow cake didn't die out with the sixties.

December Solstice

The bright log hisses in the winter fire.
Let's go down to the graves again.
It's the shortest day of the year, the darkest night.
Wooden stakes sprout in broken hearts.

Let's go down to the graves again.
At Selborne, the yew spreads its wings against
    the sky.
One by one, the women are dying.
Poisoned water, poisoned air, poisoned arrows.

It's the longest night of the year.
In churchyards, roots and bones embrace.
Even the stone heart sprouts.
The green log hisses in the liquid flame.
Let's go down to the graves again.

Elegy in the Flesh
for lc

But when I saw you tightened around your skull
as if your will were the one stretched thing
holding you together and all your remaining

life squeezed down into your swollen hand so that
John Singer Sargent, painter of mortal flesh,
red ear and forehead sunburn line

could have gotten you to a T, Elsie,
I remembered the body of my mother's mother
laid out like wax at Madame Tussaud's and I said

no, not you (*Where am I going?*), not you
nor me nor any: wood stork, mug wort—
(*Is this the journey?*)—peonies neither

in bloom nor out—
(*Aren't I supposed to be catching a train?*)—
cashew, lilac, snail darter, daffodils

beaming in your so-called living room
—(*I tried to stay*)—
spring rushing in so as not to be too late—

*

I had grown so used to your being sick,
long silences when you couldn't write or call.
This could be one of those.

*

As if putting on your skin, changing into
your new invisibility, myself an x-ray
of myself, empty

pockets, buttonholes like sockets
the heavens can be seen through, surreal, electric.
"Shall I say how it is in your clothes?" Like touch

or more like the memory of touch, silken
shadows through a yellow window, light falling
short of the lonely sidewalk.

I didn't expect to miss you half this much.
What curtain is it, Elsie, tissue-thin, that parts
and cannot part us, earth-colored

blouse I bear like a trophy
out of the dark interior, stuffed with my life.
We have covered each other's bones,

dear friend, we are one body.
As if love, too, were a kind of modesty
held up against the naked truth.

Where Were You

I was walking the dog.
I was washing the dishes.
I was coming back from lunch.
I was going to lunch.
I was in the bookstore. People were whispering.
I was walking across campus.
I was in arithmetic. They handed Mrs. Loesser a note.
I was four years old.
I wasn't born yet.
The Senegalese would come to our bungalow, shake hands,
    stand around a few minutes, shake our hands
    again and leave.
Everything stopped.
I was coming up out of a manhole. This lady was standing
    on the corner, crying.
I was on an airplane on my way to Japan.
We were driving to New Haven for the Yale game.
It was the saddest Thanksgiving.
I just prayed it wasn't a black man who did it.
I was supposed to go out to dinner.
I was at the movies. The lights came on.
I was in Vietnam.
I was putting the baby down for a nap.
I was rehearsing.
I was in a motel room. It had an orange shag rug and an
    olive green bedspread.
We were supposed to be having some meetings we thought
    were important.
I was buying a necklace I never wear anymore.
I was playing hooky.

I was swabbing the deck.
I was meeting with Rolando Cubela.
I was putting the magazine to bed.
I was crossing the border.
It was evening.
It was morning.
It was mid-day.
It was night.
I was having my nails done.
I was taking an order from this guy who wanted his toast
    toasted just on one side.
I was paying the phone bill.
I heard the word "shot."
My daughter was getting married.
I was selling Fuller brushes. This lady opened the door in
    her bathrobe. She was sobbing. Well, I thought
    to myself, that's a new one.
I was sharpening pencils.
I was reading *Life* magazine on the bus.
My grandmother said I don't want to live in this world
    anymore.
We were playing poker.
We were playing pool.
We were playing cowboys and Indians.
I was changing the sheets.
I was changing a light bulb.
I was changing my clothes.
I was changing a twenty.
I was changing lanes.
It was my last day at work.
It was payday.
I was watching TV.
I ordered a drink.

I called my mother.
Everybody stood around so they could hear the radio.
I turned on TV.
I turned the TV on.
I turned on TV.
I turned on TV.
I turned the TV on.

Grief

(Which) on the sidewalk,
white petals from pear branches,
(is) snow falling (which).

What Happened After What Happened

Pam arrived safely.
We could see it from our window.
Stay on the roof. We're coming to get you.
My boss said you're my only waitress who lives in
    Manhattan. Can you get up here?
It's difficult to get through, both by land and cell.
Thousands of papers. Like ticker-tape, like messages.
Upon returning from voting about 8:55 AM.
When I got here, I was still shaking.
All of us rushed to the hospital to be ready for the injured.
I took the baby to the park.
We watched guys playing soccer and somebody practicing
    their fly-fishing skills.
As visibility increased and I could now see the blue sky,
    there was nothing but blue sky.
Thank you for your message.
Jeff spent Tuesday taking his army physical. He had a
    perfect score.
I left the window cracked open when I went to work.
Like the ruins of a Gothic cathedral.
According to one, the stock market drops about 5% on
    average but rallies afterward.
It is very common for people to react in a variety of ways.
Plaster of Paris.
I never liked those buildings anyway.
A lot of cars parked at our end of the ferry have never been
    picked up.

New York: The Argument of Her Booke

No, she wasn't the least bit
beautiful, though she might have been beautiful
once, when young, when slim, when then and only then
because. Shoulder-length dollar signs of starched
once-blonde hair framed her long, starched, once-blonde
 face
thrust out like an elbow, yes, sharp, the best defense.
Her skin was shopworn but unlifted, and her lipstick, no,
not flattering, too orange, mostly
gone and ill-defined at the outline, spilling
unchecked into the cracks around her urban mouth.
Her eyes didn't have that much sky in them either,
and she wore, of course, black, though black is the hardest
color at the throat, where her scallop-edged shawl hugged
her broad shoulders, as if somebody short were holding her
hostage, or mugging her from behind. Below
her black slacks, she had stuffed her swollen feet
into sheer black stockings and low black leather pumps
and as she got up, yes, I noticed her chunky,
over-sized, gold-tone earrings, the strong, long,
very red nails of the hand she used to push
the stubborn bus door open, no, no
wedding but a gaudy topaz ring, and yes, it came to me
clear as a bell and loud as the harbor's lifted lamp, like her
I'm staying, both because and despite, yes, put.

Thirteen Ways of Looking at Mrs. Blackbird

I
She and her turtledove of twenty years

II
Share a nest of offices at Fifth and 103rd

III
They've built from scratch.

IV
He's a psychiatrist. She's a millionaire

V
Who makes seed grants from her own private tax-exempt foundation.

VI
They fly uptown together each morning;

VII
Evenings and weekends they devote to their four children.

VIII
From her perch she looks down on lawn parties, charity balls.

IX
Every day she pecks at a brown bag lunch in the local pocket park;

X
There are no good bird-feeders in this habitat.

XI
She claims she learns more from her poor chickadees

XII
Than they do from her: Win-win, win-win, win-win,

XIII
She bullies and coos.

Not Nearly the Sonnet She'd Have Written Herself

I went to college with Edna St. Vincent Millay.
Or, not exactly: fifty years before,
She lived in the room above me in the tower,
And threw herself, for effect, from the window bay,
Or threatened to. Or so they say.
She was nothing if not dramatic. Since that hour
Many a difficult woman has followed the now-or-
Never dare of her great poems. They
Made our mothers and grandmothers gay.
We too have felt that pressure on the spine,
Her thrill of sex, self-pity, pain and power
And mind. She runs, like blood, in the family.
Fell down and died beside a glass of wine,
Or so they say. It isn't true, however.

Sally Field Has a Dream about Her Mother

I'm in my kitchen dressed in red
blouse, red skirt, red shoes, red polish
on my toes and fingernails, red lipstick
(in real life only my friend Marion can do this,
find the exact right shade of matching lipstick),
when in walks you know who, who wouldn't
be caught dead in red alive, but now that she can
do anything she wants to, *voilà*!
                              your total scarlet woman
right down to the hooves. She does it to outdo me.
She does it to be sexier, and tall. In real life
I could kiss the top of her head, but not in her current
incarnation. Am I dreaming or could it be
she does it to be like me, because *she likes me!*
Members of the Academy, I'm blushing,
is it hot in here? I don't know who to thank first.

Double Take

Tom has turned the mike away,
"Can you hear me in back?"
and when we answer yes, begins:

I dreamed my friend got up and walked;
he was taller than me
and ... Halfway through

just as he's saying
and now he's dead, whom I loved.
He was a poet ... a maintenance man

walks out from the wings,
swings the mike back beneath Tom's chin
and walks completely off again,

who has another audience he's thinking of,
or is. Rueful, Tom begins again
amplified, alive, amused.

Almost Biblical

The wind was blowing so hard today!
The sky bright blue again, but the air more humid.
There were whitecaps in the harbor. It was Wednesday,

A day like any other day,
Except no planes were flying overhead.
The wind was blowing so hard today

A small fishing boat capsized in the bay,
Killing its owner, Victor Amesquita; his three companions,
    injured.
There were whitecaps in the harbor. It was Wednesday

All day. The names lifted away even as they
Were spoken. It was almost Biblical, Marion said.
The wind was blowing so hard today

A tree limb fell on thirteen New Jersey teenagers,
A construction worker was knocked out by a piece of
    winged plywood.
There were whitecaps in the harbor. It was Wednesday:

Gusts were stronger than on any but two or three days
A year. Damage was exceptionally widespread.
The wind was blowing so hard today
There were whitecaps in the harbor; but at least it wasn't
    Tuesday. It was Wednesday.

New York City
September 11, 2002

How High Is the Sky

White cloths billow
from tenth story beams
like Marilyn's skirts
above a subway grate,
cool sheets fanning
a child's sickbed,
snapping fingers
of flags flying
into this wide open,
under construction morning.

Louise Glück's Hair

If I keep your cuttings from the salon floor.
   If they burn, if I breathe their bones and smoke.
      If I wind them in my pubic hair.

If I weave with them an inheritable cloak.
   If I glue them to the scalp of voodoo Barbie.
      If that's not a stroke

Of genius. If I compare them to a summer's day.
   If I finger them like coins in my copper pocket.
      If they bring me luck. If in the fair reliquary

Of their art, they break into lines, if they catch the light.
   If I analyze their exact genetic composition.
      If I count their feet.

If theirs is the logic of life's condition:
   I.e., if split ends, what split beginnings;
      From black roots, what brittle, bleached conclusion.

If I master the syntax of sweepings.
   If, in a meadow, I let the sky take them.
      If it plays them like strings.

If they whiten with time.
   In winter, if they crystallize
      When wet. If they rhyme.

In their disappearing ink, if I revise and revise.
   If when I occupy the barber's chair.
      If words like lockets save our brunettish lives.

Cut Short

Next I'll have it stripped and dyed
    turquoise, like that girl at the Tate,
        her whole head a halo, glowing.

My daughter says as long as I don't look like a guy.
    I promise big earrings, plenty of make-up.
        I'm 52 and 1/3, going on 53,

when my mother died. I tell my friends
    to look out for me, I might step in front of a truck.
        You're not supposed to outlast your own mother

the first time, let alone twice.
    She killed herself by mistake. It was a natural
        reaction, getting my hair cut

short, like a nun
    or Joan of Arc, her all-time favorite, a disguise
        to slip between enemy lines

my unacknowledged dream of freedom. I'm afraid
    I'm giving up my femininity
        for nothing. Bob-headed Carrington

shot herself at 38. She said oh,
    to have the ambition of Tintoretto and to paint
        like a diseased dormouse. My friend Marion

tells me don't worry, my hair
    will grow long as art in the grave
        where all of us will be the same age.

How Much Do I Love You

The old gent lives in a six-story townhouse.
Art deco bronze-work adorns his glass front door.
My dog and I overtake him every morning
on his way to Mass. He shuffles his slippers,
raises his hat. We stop to chat.
This morning, he gave me his name, Homer Butler,
like a watch piece he's a little nervous about trusting
to a favorite, impetuous niece.

Good Friday in Umbria

Then everybody's suddenly ascending
but me: for me it's the bottoms of feet, hems of gowns,
a cumulus Renaissance ceiling, dark undersides
of women's breasts (but pink nipples), nostrils, jawbones,
white wingtips rising

into the blue della Robbia blue
of the broken Madonna and child I've just dropped,
one clean line driven like lightning between them.
My mother's dead. My daughter is losing her virginity.
It sounds funny.

*

I break the surface of the water, diving in.
It's a shock, the pleasure the body takes
in forgetting: gravity, the parts of speech, the need
for breathing on one's own. Water
strokes every hair of my skin, fills every hungry crevice and
    spills
like more than you'll ever know what to do with
down my sides, between my thighs, off my strong brown
    arms.
You should see how beautiful I am from this angle.

*

Later, after five, when the monastery bells
have called the nuns to prayer
and the stores in this part of the country reopen, we buy
    glue
so strong American construction workers

hang from the bottoms of 2x4s and cranes
and airplane wings, oh, Icarus!
We can stick this mother to this child
so fast it will almost seem as if nothing ever happened.

*

That boy who showed us his *presepio*,
when he switched on the light
and the scratchy record started up again

and the angels on their squeaky wheel
lurched around the manger as the daylight dawned
and grew and faded, the yellow lights

of the hilltowns shone out from their walls
and the firelights flickered and the lanterns
of the peasants on their separate journeys

pointed to that hill and the daylight dawned
and grew and faded above them where the young man hung
and the mother of the young man lay:

Mother of God, weren't you angry?
Didn't you hate him for leaving you,
even though, even though you knew, you knew?

Didn't you want to cover him with kisses,
didn't you want to make him stay?
Mary, didn't you miss him?

*

Afterwards, we lie naked beside the pool.
We can still feel the hands of the wind god caress us,
the hot sun's powerful rays that fall on us, sinners
and saviors alike. We are born,
small birds, out of our own broken hearts,
out of the blue beforehand of our ignorance,
with a cry to rend cloth or shatter clay,
curtains of flesh like water parting
to let us in.

What Big Teeth

> (In Anticipation of Becoming a Grandmother
> Sometime in the Unforeseeable Future)

I'll fly out.
   Skinny lips, flapping ears, four eyes
      redoubled in a brand new buddy boy. Her

eyebrows, sharp chin, his father's penis—looks
   unfamiliar to me—my sense of humor. My mother told
      me
   twenty years younger she'd have married my first
      husband

herself. I'll take the house next door. My daughter needs me.
   When it turns out she can't have children, I'll do it
      for her. When it turns out he doesn't make her happy,

I'll take her back,
   rub her back, make her swell with pleasure.
      That's how a woman gets pregnant. When she goes
         to sleep

the way she used to when she was a baby,
   I'll wrap her in sable, my arms, the receiving blanket.
      Eat the placenta warm. I need my strength.

from *What's Wrong*

Under the Covers

Certain nights
When the pillow fit just right under my neck,
When the flashlight tucked under my chin stayed tucked,
The novel on my knees stayed propped up
And my parents had somebody over,

When the world was well-bred
And the heroine was young, and the moon hung yellow
And perfectly round on the page that explained
What everything meant:

Then it was heaven on the second floor,
In the corner bedroom, in the one twin bed,
Under the bedspread and the blankets and the pure
One hundred percent cotton sheet

Made in this country before the war.
Plots thickened. They don't do that anymore.
Characters lived. In the ventilated air
Their voices could almost be heard
Downstairs, talking things over.

Friggins Division

Did you dare glass
to see if it shatters the way air shatters?
did you stare noon blind, or stand
on the shoulders of cliffs to find out who, you
or the wind was taller?

Which day did the family decide?
on the day you tried if it wouldn't be just as easy
breathing through skin? or did they infer
from the red, just the red risk of your hair
you must be mad?

When you noticed the sky
congeal in their faces like so much fat, was it that
you laughed at, or the padded cell
or the good good sense of the personnel
plucking at bobby pins?

All that night
not hank by hank, but hair by individual hair
did you yank it out, root,
earth, heaven, and all
to see if it made any difference?

Skate

Off-
balance, into the wide wide world
she's going to wow
on one foot:
she always does things the hard way. Down
of course, her mother imagines
her long bones breaking, her long
convalescence.
          No harm done. It's twilight,
there's music, a woman
holding her daughter's shoes in her lap
and ice almost exactly the color of medals.
But not yet.

Found Poem

next time
you yell at me like that
i mite run away from home
and that goes for
Daddy too

if i run
away from home
i'll leve you a note
saying ware i'll be
Thank you

Doomed

The road sign reads Kansas, another example
of language imitating life. The land's so flat
the wind acts as if it would like to blow you to hell, but
you're modern, this is it: a wheat field

is a wheat field
is a wheat field till you wish. Be careful.
This is that dead stretch they warned you
to cross at night. They were right. If you're driving
straight through to the Coast, you're both crazy
by this time, you are not quite the strangers you
may have been when you left.
Neither of you has ever been this far west.

Your companion pops No-Doz, flips the radio dial
every few minutes to make sure he is
where he thinks he is, no fool
like the deejays spinning blind in their booths.
Every station repeats the same news.
You swear you can smell the sea
and he loves it, no question
California, the two of you, the future

you've heard a hundred times before. It's a hit
and it shines on the other side of this landscape
like the light from the setting sun or a star, traveling
at the same speed you are.

Someplace Hot

Boats out
under a sky as blue as my baby's eyes and so
deep she's drowning: not a cloud in sight.

Anything that pure, pure
enough to float—like ice, the hard light
making progress impossible, a trap, behind

the smiling snapshot of a face—your face
scares me it's so fine. It cuts
into my dreams and saves me, me and the children

for another time. Help. Day dawns
thick and stupid as quicksand.
I reach for a cigarette.

Someplace hot, somebody's about to get shot.
I'm probably pregnant. I'm the only one here
who looks sick when you say the insurance

covers every imaginable disaster.

Next Time

Nothing so melodramatic.
At first you won't even notice the tremor
when one of us speaks, or the hair-line cracks
in the light between us: then watching it crumble
takes days you can't take your eyes off
the way some people can't see through a screen

or prefer not to. I wear gray
to blur at a distance, assuming I get that far
and no make-up to make it look interesting. Then I go
little by little, testing the air for anger, your eyes
widening, the ground could give way. If you call me

back, I'll deny what I'm doing
as you knew I would. We're safe with each other.
Even at night: we stand by the window together
as the last little pieces of light fly apart, and we talk.
I agree with whatever it is you were saying.

What's Wrong

Even the light, exhausted
hours before it reaches the horizon, crawls up each morning
over the edge and collapses

flat out. Like a lung. It's February.
People are cold and unsympathetic. They want the sun
to set an example, bright, on time,

everyone doing the jobs they were hired to do.
This is the wrong time of year to talk reasons.
If a woman sleeps through

the alarm and the phone calls and the husband trying
to bring her to: to what? The world
is a sickness we succumb to daily, our own need

pulling us in. It takes courage
to listen to the details, what's the food like,
how does the routine work in this place,
where's the other way out.

Rules of the Contest

Deadline is September 30.
Postmark no later than midnight that date.
Include a brief biography.

One entry only.
No age or other limit.
Deadline is September 30.

To insure impartiality
List name, address, and phone number on separate sheet.
Include a brief biography.

Any
Degrees, honors, grants: please state.
Deadline is September 30.

Theme: mortality.
Any form. Any length.
Include a brief biography:

Tell why.
Decisions final. Prize immediate.
Deadline is September 30.
Include a brief biography.

from *The Papers Said*

Landscape Painting

I used to think the sun was going down
(the light's ambiguous, so the time of day's not clear).
Now I'm starting to believe it's really dawn.

Because the picture's always been around
I never looked this carefully before.
I used to think the sun was going down

when, actually, the lights would be coming up
in the two houses, then—and no lights appear.
So I'm starting to believe it's really dawn

and everyone's still sound
asleep, though the sky's growing yellower and yellower.
I used to think the sun was going down

because the silence looks so utterly profound,
nothing to break it but the birds and the brook's dark
    murmur.
But I'm starting to believe it's really dawn.

Ironic, isn't it, death should be the reason.
Young and melancholy, sure I'd live forever,
I used to think the sun was going down.
Now I'm starting to believe it's really dawn.

For Gregory, Chuck and John

Not like skin cloddishly dripping off the bone
Of the A-bomb victim or the unrecognizable man
Who's lost too much weight too fast;
Not like the prow of a woman's face in the wind,
Wrinkles splayed back to the blue-black hairline,
Mouth clamped in a facelift's ferocious grin;
But so gradual, so slow, so long a degradation
The skin had time to scale itself down,
To thin, to adjust
To the daylight shining through the petals
Of the white peonies in the bedroom.
They were so beautiful, diaphanous as chiffon.
One day a breeze came up in the conversation.
We turned to speak of it, but you were gone.

The Papers Said

In Kenya they have two paved highways.
Commuters throw garbage out the window to baboons
so used to being fed this way
they wait at intervals like pets or trashcans.
One day a man threw out an orange
he'd filled with chili powder just for the hell of it

to see what would happen (it
rolled in the red dust at the highway's
edge) because the man hated those fucking baboons
or whatever the word is in Swahili, the way
they jerk off at the side of the road, or show their
          disgusting red cans
to each other, and this one not especially orange

orange
got picked up by one of those fuckers, who pushed it
into his mouth and bit down. The white man in the green
          car on the liquid red highway
under the burning blue sky (or whatever the baboon
word is for hellfire)—the man in the green car went his way.
Baboons scream as only baboons can.

The man felt merciful: no more living trashcans.
He forgave his wife. As the sky turned the brilliant orange
of an African sunset, he drove home. It
gratified him to see the sides of the highway
deserted, the entire baboon
population he'd driven away.

For a while, he went out of his way

to be nice to his wife and children. He let them watch
    American
T.V.; on the weekend he bought a six-pack of orange
pop, packed it
in the car and took them all for a drive along the highway.
Of course the baboons

were back; he expected that. *Baboon
Attacks*, however, he did not expect, especially the way
it seemed to recognize the green car (uncanny,
the papers called it), hurled itself at the open window when
    an orange
shape glistened briefly there, and ripped the man's throat
    out. Call it
whatever you like, poetic justice, but people aren't safe on
    the nation's highways,

the papers said.

Radio

No radio
in car

No radio on board

No radio
Already stolen

Absolutely no radio!

Radio broken
Alarm is set
To go off

No radio
No money

No radio
No valuables

No radio or
valuables
in car or trunk

No radio
Stolen 3X

No radio
Empty trunk

Empty glove compartment
Honest

In car
Nothing of value

No radio
No nuthin
(No kidding)

Radio Broken
Nothing Left!

Radio Gone
Note Hole in Dashboard

Warning!
Radio Will Not Play
When Removed
Security Code Required

Would you keep
Anything valuable
In this wreck?

No valuables
In this van

Please do not
Break-in
Unnecessarily

Thank you
For your kind
Consideration

Nothing of value
in car
No radio
No tapes
No telephone

Complaint

No matter how much,
As soon as I tell him
I want him, I need him,
Ho hum.

As soon as I tell him
I want to be touched,
Where I want to be touched
Goes numb.

The Man Who Used to Live
in My Apartment

Are the shelves, he wants to know, *still there?*
and describes in detail the dark walk-in closet where
I keep my off-season clothes, dormant poinsettias,
boxes to ship things back in, birdcages, diaries,
eyes of newt, peace posters. Who is this thane,

this friend of a friend, sitting next to me now
on the train back into the city, asking
how did you solve the rounded window problem? shades
that pull up from the bottom, I tell him
as if it was any of his business:

I hardly ever pull them up. We change the subject.
Kitchen, bedroom, bedroom, bath: he haunts me
like Banquo's ghost, persistent, pushy, dying to repossess
the apartment. I can't make the closet door stay shut.
Inside, a ruckus like an argument

erupting: pipes burst, walls crumble, blue sky
    shows through,
weeds, frogs, roof tiles, poppies and buttercups!
A satin strap slides off one shoulder like a sigh
when he calls three days later to say *how bout lunch*
because there's so much he feels we have in common.

No is the Answer, the Answer is No

Then your shoulder or your head or your whole body
collides with a wall of bricks, the pain
so dazzling the remotest memories of your childhood
flare up like faces

when a match is struck in the dark, a glimpse
of your own quick shadow on the cave wall
and all the names you call out to come back, come back
hollow, the smell of sulfur on their breath; or else

a door opens and you rush in, so surprised
by your forward momentum you wince
to find yourself intact and standing
in the room you wanted so badly to stand it—

empty, bare white, no windows, no secrets,
two doors and a ladder-back chair with a rush seat
planted in the middle of the floor. This is your life.
It makes you want to throw up. The door

back to where you came from stands open, darkness
hot in your face, somebody laughing, a whole history
    of failure
you'd really rather not include in this story.
Do you know who that voice is? Old flame

Mr. Muse, Sinatra-smooth, two cigarettes in an ashtray
burning, tempting you
to confuse the messenger with the message
it takes a lifetime

to translate into usable language: Shoot.
Take a shit. Take voice. Take flying lessons.
Say slough of despond twice with a straight face.
Write rhymed verse

so accessible it makes you suspect
among poets and pet lovers alike. Relax
in the lonely chair your father left you,
the needlepoint chair handed down to you by your mother,

the crooked chair van Gogh painted of himself
when he was almost happy. These are your instruments
of torture and deliverance, your Book of Kells, the skeleton
key in the heart-shaped lock. Twist it

however you like, it opens: you cannot escape
your freedom. That second door might still, don't you
    think,
lead to an absolutely sun-struck patio, fragrant mountains
by the sea, red geraniums—look! the light

is bulging at the door,
longing to engulf you and carry you away
to heaven, I'm in heaven, like poor old, dear old
dead Fred Astaire, dancing up and down the rungs of his
    chair.

Notes

page 16: General Curtis LeMay proposed bat-bombs as a means to create more firestorms in Japan, like that of Tokyo, at the end of World War II, in the event that the atom bombs at Hiroshima and Nagasaki did not convince the Emperor to surrender.

page 27: "Shall I say how it is in your clothes" is quoted from Maxine Kumin's elegy for Anne Sexton, "How It Is."

page 29: Rolando Cubela was a CIA contact in the U.S. government scheme to assassinate Fidel Castro during the early 1960s.

page 38: Lines in italics are quoted from "Elegy for Robert Winner" by Thomas Lux.

page 42: Dora Carrington (1893-1932), British artist, killed herself shortly after the death of her long-time companion, Lytton Strachey, the author, most famously, of *Eminent Victorians*.

page 52: Friggins Division is the name of the psychiatric ward of a New Orleans hospital where Tennessee Williams was once confined.

About the Author

Laurel Blossom is the author of three previous books of poetry, *The Papers Said*, *What's Wrong*, and *Any Minute* (a chapbook.). She has been the recipient of fellowships from the National Endowment for the Arts, the New York Foundation for the Arts, the Ohio Arts Council, and Harris Manchester College (Oxford University) among others. Her award-winning poems have appeared widely in literary journals and anthologies, both in print and online. She is co-founder of The Writers Community, the esteemed writing residency and workshop program that is now part of the YMCA National Writer's Voice. Her book-length poem, *Degrees of Latitude*, is forthcoming.

More at www.laurelblossom.com